© **High-Level Corruption, Cynthia Gabriel's Reception of Death Threats, the Enforced Disappearance & Gruesome Murder of Altantuya Sharibuu by TWO (2) Police Bodyguards to the then Deputy Prime Minister & Defence Minister, the present Prime Minister of Malaysia, NAJIB RAZAK : The Scorpene and Arms Corruption Scandal & the Altantuya Sharibuu Tragedy**

Enforced disappearance takes place when a person is arrested, detained, abducted or otherwise deprived of their liberty by government officials or by organized groups or private individuals whose actions are condoned by the government in some way.

This is followed by a refusal to disclose the fate or whereabouts of the persons concerned, placing them outside the protection of the law. Enforced disappearance is a crime under international law, prohibited by the Rome Statute of the International Criminal Court and the International Convention for the Protection of All Persons from Enforced Disappearance, among other international standards.

Enforced disappearance is a dehumanizing practice which has long-lasting and damaging consequences for both the disappeared person and his or her families and loved ones. It is a particularly cruel human rights abuse because it is of a continuous nature, particularly for families and loved ones of the victim who often wait for years to learn the truth about the victim's fate.

Every year Amnesty International also joins activists around the world to observe 30 August as the International Day of the Disappeared, to remember those who have disappeared and their relatives.

On October 18, 2006, a pretty young Mongolian translator named Altantuya Shaariibuu was brutally murdered at the age of 28. Her mutilated body was found in a jungle clearing near the Kuala Lumpur suburb of Sha Alam. Her reputation has been brutalized as well. The pictures printed here may give some of her back to the world.

After her remains were found about a month after the murder, Altantuya's accused killers, Abdul Razak Baginda, her former lover and the head of a politically well-connected think tank, and two bodyguards for Deputy Prime Minister Najib Tun Razak, were arrested almost immediately in a blaze of newspaper headlines that all but convicted them.

She had also worked as Abdul Razak's translator on a shady deal he was brokering for the Malaysian government to buy submarines from France. The pair seem to have travelled to Paris together. A letter found after she was killed appeared to be a demand for money from him for the care of her child, which he may have fathered. She was last seen by eyewitnesses getting into a car outside Abdul Razak's house with the two elite bodyguards. Abdul Razak had requested help in dealing with her vocal demands for money and presence at the house.

The trial has now been underway for six months while prosecutors wade through a tangle of jurisdictional disputes and take testimony from a tedious list of tangential witnesses. Both prosecution and defense seem intent on keeping the obvious political ramifications of the trial out of the courtroom. It almost seems as if the trial is being delayed just to lessen the impact of a mistrial or even the acquittal of the politically prominent defendants.

In the meantime, Altantuya's name has been dragged through the mud for so long that she almost has ceased to exist as a person. After being identified by local newspapers following the murder, she was first characterized as a part-time model (code language for a high-priced call girl). She also has been reviled for being an unwed mother, and for jet-setting to Europe with Abdul Razak. She has been described as a bitter, spurned lover demanding money from her rich boyfriend. Her family, meanwhile, has said she worked hard and was just trying to find her way in life.

In a letter found after her death (spelling corrected), she sounds like any jilted young woman: "To see your lover is nothing criminal right? Yes (I) was in shock. I wrote some stupid letters to him where I said I kill myself I want help. Yes I try to blackmail him. Maybe it's my fault but no I really understand he doesn't love me anymore and I need to stop that I asked money from him to go back how he promised to me. He lied to me to help and ruin my life. I came to KL to see him to face to face and ask why acting like that. Maybe rich person and he got family doing this. But when I come I did some thing stupid I write letter where I said I will kill myself and thing like that."

And, she adds: "They say Malaysia is different from Mongolia and said they know people in police so can easy put me to jail. If in Malaysia law goes like that I can't complain. But true is I did nothing to him. I'm just normal girl trying to meet my lover who lied to me and promised many things but now wants to put me in jail or kill."

From a series of pictures made available to Asia Sentinel by Syed Abdul Rahman AlHabshi, the honorary Mongolian Consul General in Malaysia, Altantuya looks like nothing more than an attractive young woman off on the trip of her life to Europe. AlHabshi declined a request to say where the pictures came from but they are believed to have been found among her possessions after she was killed. She looks happy. Perhaps she was with her lover when these were taken. Her family has declined to elaborate on the circumstances of the pictures.

According to trial testimony by Burmaa Oyunchimeg, Altantuya's cousin, who accompanied the victim to Kuala Lumpur to attempt to get Abdul Razak to give her money, there was one more picture. It depicted Altantuya having dinner with Abdul Razak and Deputy Prime Minister Najib. The picture was not in her possession when her decomposed body was found last October. The court has made no attempt to find the picture and Najib has not been called as a witness by either side.

ALIRAN article : Scorpene scandal surfaces in French court; Suaram vindicated - dated 29 Jan 2016

(http://aliran.com/civil-society-voices/2016-civil-society-voices/scorpene-scandal-resurfaces-suaram-vindicated/)

After six long years of investigations, this first indictment of the arms maker shows that Suaram's suspicion of commissions paid to Malaysian officials in the Scorpene deal is well founded, says Kua Kia Soong.

The Scorpene submarines scandal involving suspected commissions paid to Malaysian defence officials in the French submarines sale in 2002 has finally surfaced in the French court with a first indictment issued against the former boss of an international subsidiary of Thales, suspected of having corrupted then defence minister and the present Malaysian Prime Minister Najib Razak.

Bernard Baiocco, the former president of Thales International Asia (Thint Asia) was indicted before magistrate Roger Le Loire on 15 December or "active bribery of foreign public officials" including Najib Razak, then minister of defense, and one of his advisers, Abdul Razak Baginda, according to the news agency AFP.

Suaram's complaint to the French in November 2009 had started a preliminary inquiry and a judicial investigation opened in Paris in

2012. Searches by the French police at Thales and DCNS offices had led to the seizure of numerous documents.

After six long years of investigations, this first indictment of the arms maker shows that Suaram's suspicion of commissions paid to Malaysian officials in the Scorpene deal is well founded and we have been vindicated.

The sale of two Scorpene submarines and a sub Marino Agosta to Malaysia was the most expensive military procurement by Malaysia to date, costing nearly RM5bn for the hardware plus more than RM2bn for the training of operatives and maintenance of the submarines.

The French judges have been examining contracts which they suspect of being used to pay for bribes. One of these, referred to as "C5 commercial engineering" involved payment of 30m euros by DCNI, a subsidiary of DCN to Thales International Asia, in respect of "selling expenses for export".

The French judicial investigations also show that another company, Terasasi, whose main shareholder Razak Baginda, then adviser to the defence minister, Najib Razak, was paid almost the same amount for consultations. Investigators suspect these so-called "consultations" to be a front for bribes.

In the investigations, another contract provided for the payment of 114m euros to the Malaysian company Perimekar, the main contractor of the Scorpene deal.

All this time, the Malaysian government has not told parliament or the public about the existence of Terasasi (Abdul Razak Baginda's other company) and that it had a share of the spoils from the purchase of the submarines. The government has only tried to justify the payments to Perimekar.

The existence of Terasasi and payments it received only emerged when the French prosecutors' documents came to light. It is time the Malaysian government reveals the role that Terasasi played in the Scorpene deal.

The Scorpene scandal has been fueled by the gruesome murder of Mongolian intermediary, Altantuya Shaariibuu, in 2006. According to the testimony of Razak Baginda's private investigator, Altantuya, was allegedly the mistress of Abdul Razak Baginda.

In an article by Emma Reynolds in NEWS.COM.AU dated SEPTEMBER 22, 2015

(http://www.news.com.au/lifestyle/real-life/true-stories/malaysias-most-explosive-murder-mystery-is-blowing-up-in-australia/news-story/d8e92bbd5172292a63664f90e2598767)

Altantuya was taken from Baginda's home on the night of her murder. A week later, the defence analyst was detained along with the two officers later convicted of the crime, and charged with abetting the murder.

It is alleged that Altantuya was far more than just his mistress, and had assisted in a controversial submarine deal thought to have been used for kickbacks. Some claim she was pregnant with his child.

Baginda brokered Malaysia's billion-dollar purchase of two Scorpene submarines from France in 2002, and the $US125 million contract for coordinating the building of the subs went to companies reportedly set up by Baginda in his wife's name.

He claimed he didn't meet Altantuya until 2004, but receipts uncovered by a French investigation show she travelled with him to Paris, Hong Kong and Macau.

Cynthia Gabriel, director of an anti-corruption organisation in Malaysia, insists his girlfriend would have at least known about the deal. Gabriel has since received death threats.

This February, he spoke from detention to say that he had been "under orders" and "the important people with motive are still free."

In a published article by SUARAM JB dated 11 January 2010, here :

(http://suaramjb1.blogspot.my/2010/11/submarine-scandal-and-altantuya-murder.html)

The Submarine Scandal and the Altantuya Murder

11/01/2010 SUARAM JB

THE SUBMARINE SCANDAL AND THE ALTANTUYA MURDER

by Cynthia Gabriel

The defence ministry has spent more than one billion euros or about RM 7.3 billion of the rakyat's money for the purchase of the two submarines, which are reportedly of questionable quality. The first submarine, the KD Tuanku Abdul Rahman could not sink in tropical waters, while the second arrived more than 7 months after the scheduled date of arrival.

· Adding intrigue and mystery to this controversial deal was the mysterious and horrifying death in 2006, by two policemen closely linked to then deputy prime minister Najib Razak. The deceased is a Mongolian national, believed to be a translator and mistress of Abdul Razak Baginda, a political analyst, also closely linked to najib.

· C4 explosives were said to have killed her. This explosive is not easily available in the market. It is available only in the Defence ministry and normally used for demolishing buildings. Who issued the explosives to be used and why? When Altantuya was killed, Najib was still the Defence Minister.

Who is Altantuya Shaariibuu?

· Shaariibuugiin Altantuyaa (1978 – 2006), is a Mongolian national, who was murdered brutally in Shah Alam Malaysia on the 19th October 2006, during the month of Ramadhan.

· She worked as a translator for Mr. Abdul Razak Baginda, who is a well-known political analyst, a close ally to Prime Minister Najib Razak.

· When Altantuya Shaariibuu was killed, Najib was the deputy prime minister and defense minister.

· She was also a single mother with two young children below 10 years old.

· Her younger son has a rare brain disease and she was trying to earn enough money to send him for a good medical treatment.

· Now both her sons are orphaned and they are taken care of by their grandfather – Mr Setev Shaariibuu and his spouse in a village in Mongolia.

· Altantuya was recruited for the job because she was reportedly fluent in Mongolian, Russian, Chinese, English, and some French. In fact prior to this job, she has had some business dealings with Abdul Razak.

· Razak Baginda was at that time, a defense analyst from the Malaysian Strategic Research Centre think-tank.

Who killed Altantuya?

· On 9 April 2009, the Shah Alam High Court meted out the death sentence to two accused – policemen Chief Inspector Azilah Hadri and Corporal Sirul Azhar.

· They had been members of the elite Unit Tindakan Khas (the Malaysian Police Special Action Force or counter-terrorism unit) and were both assigned to the office of the Deputy Prime Minister Najib Tun Razak, who was also the Defence Minister at the time of the murder.

· The duo were bodyguards of Najib who was then DPM. The trial took 159 days. Both policemen never knew Altantuya and until today, the questions remain:

· What is their motive for killing her?

· Who ordered her killing?

· These questions were never answered. Another accused was Abdul Razak Baginda, but he escaped the gallows and was released without his defence being called.

· On 31 October 2008 the High Court acquitted Abdul Razak Baginda of abetment in the murder of Altantuya, with the prosecution saying they would appeal the acquittal. To date, the appeal has yet to transpire.

Where and how was she killed?

· Altantuya was murdered by large quantities of C-4 explosives, large enough to bring down a four-storey building. The remnants of her body was found in a jungle clearing in Puncak Shah Alam.

· C4 explosives is not the kind you can find in a 7-11 store or a grocery store. In other words, it is not easily accessible. In fact, it is learnt, that C4 explosives is only available if approval for its usage is given by the Ministry of Defence.

· According to court testimony by one of her murderers, Altantuya was first shot twice – one in her head and the other in her abdomen – before she was strapped to the explosives which eventually blew her into pieces.

· Altantuya was killed because she knew too much?

· That's what her dad Mr Shaariibuu said when he came to Malaysia in 2007 to attend her murder trial

· According to reports by the French newspaper Liberation, Altantuya found out that one of the parties involved in negotiations, a Spanish company Armaris, had paid out the commissions of 114 million euros for the deal (reportedly one billion euros or RM4.7 billion for the purchase of three submarines).

· The commission was credited into the accounts of a company controlled by Razak, Perimekar.

In an article by the C4CENTER.ORG.MY dated 29 January 2016, headed by the very same Cynthia Gabriel, the then SUARAM executive director who had received death threats due to her and SUARAM's endeavours in the Scorpene and Arms High-Level Corruption Scandal & the Altantuya Sharibuu gruesome murder.

The former boss of a French company accused of paying kickbacks to a former aide of Datuk Seri Najib Razak has been indicted for "active bribery of foreign public officials", according to an AFP report quoted by Malaysiakini.

The report said Bernard Baiocco, 72, former president of Thales International Asia (Thint Asia), was indicted on December 15 last year, for paying commissions to Abdul Razak Baginda, the political analyst who was acquitted of the 2006 murder of Mongolian citizen Altantuya Shaariibuu. Baiocco and a director of shipbuilder DCN International, which sold two Scorpene submarines to Malaysia in 2002, were also indicted for "complicity in misuse of corporate assets".

The news comes four years after local rights group Suaram filed a complaint with a Paris civil court in 2012 over the multi-million ringgit Scorpene scandal. Suaram had filed a suit against DCNS for allegedly paying 114.9 million euro in illegal commissions to Perimekar Sdn Bhd, a company partly owned by Razak, a close confidante of Najib, then the defence minister. Following this, French authorities raided the offices of Thales and DCN.

Cynthia Gabriel, who spearheaded efforts to bring the scandal to French courts, welcomed the news, saying "this is the moment we have been waiting for". "We feel very encouraged and happy to hear the case has moved forward and that French investigations have arrived on a very important finding and a key French official has been formally indicted. "He would have to defend himself in court and all the purchases linked to the Scorpene submarines will now be in public domain," Cynthia, who heads Center to Combat Corruption and Cronyism (C4), told Malaysiakini.

In an expose by FIDH.ORG dated 13 August 2013, the Observatory has been informed by Suara Rakyat Malaysia (SUARAM) about the harassment against Ms. Cynthia Gabriel, SUARAM Secretariat Member, allegedly in retaliation for SUARAM's role in exposing a corruption case involving the Malaysian Government and related to the Scorpene submarine scandal, involving at least RM 500 million in suspected kickbacks.

Further, in an AFP news article published in Expatica.Com.Fr, Amnesty International had accused Malaysian authorities of persecuting activists pressing a huge corruption and murder case allegedly linked to Prime Minister Najib Razak.

Highly-respected human rights organisation Suaram has alleged that a kickback worth $160 million was paid to a company linked to Abdul Razak Baginda, an associate of Najib, for a $1.1-billion submarine purchase in 2002.

(http://www.expatica.com/fr/news/Malaysia-anti-graft-activist-harassed-by-govt-Amnesty_383060.html)

In a press statement made by SUARAM (Penang) dated 30th May 2012 :

FRENCH SUBMARINES DIVING MALAYSIA INTO DEEP CONTROVERSY

30 MAY 2012

PRESS STATEMENT

FRENCH SUBMARINES DIVING MALAYSIA

INTO DEEP CONTROVERSY

SUARAM, a leading Malaysian human rights NGO, welcomes all media, both regional and Malaysian media, as well as members of the diplomatic community in Bangkok, to this exclusive press briefing, on one of the most sensational and controversial corruption scandals in our country, and perhaps in the region of ASEAN.

In a script befitting a Hollywood spy thriller, this corruption scandal surrounds the purchase of two French "SCORPENE" class submarines whose price continues to escalate till today, the shocking and brutal murder of a glamorous Mongolian woman, the blowing up of her body by C4 explosives, the decision of the French courts to hear evidence about the alleged bribery of top Malaysian and French officials – and the growing links between these – spell big headaches for the ruling administration, and e specially for current Prime Minister Najib Razak.

This is the first joint media conference between our French lawyers and the SUARAM team, following the commencement of a judicial inquiry at the Tribunal De Grande Instance in Paris, that will probe alleged corruption crimes and illegal bribes involving top officials from both Malaysia and France.

As was earlier reported, the SUARAM delegation comprising board members Kua Kia Soong, Cynthia Gabriel and Fadiah Nadwa Fikri, returned after a successful hearing before Judge Roger Le Loire, one of the two Instruction Judges assigned to oversee the case.

The Judge had principally accepted a list of seven proposed witnesses including current Defence Minister Ahmad Zahid Hamidi, former Defence Minister and current Prime Minister Najib Razak, and a central figure in the procurement process, Abdul Razak Baginda as key witnesses that can further assist in the inquiry before the Tribunal.

Access to the Investigation Papers

Following the commencement of the inquiry, SUARAM has gained full privileged access to the 153 investigation papers from the Public Prosecutor's office. This is a huge step forward, as many of the details kept confidential are now made accessible to SUARAM as the civil Plaintiff in the criminal case against the DCNS (French shipbuilding company).

French law provides several constraints on the area of access. While we are not able to obtain a hard copy and distribute copies, we are however entitled to full view of the documents and are able to quote them to the media and to the public.

It is also crucial to note that the complaint lodged by SUARAM has led to the commencement of a criminal investigation which has just opened, leaving a huge possibility of criminal prosecution of those involved in this corruption scandal. Our lawyers have forewarned that the French and Malaysian officials as well as the companies involved in the corruption scandal may be put on the "suspects" list as the criminal case proceeds in the French Courts.

Legal Jurisdiction

Malaysia's Legal Obligations under the UN Convention Against Corruption (UNCAC)

Malaysia as a signatory to the UNCAC since 2008, is now obliged to cooperate with other nation states in preventing, investigating and prosecuting offenders of corruption. State parties are bound to render specific forms of mutual legal assistance in gathering and transferring evidence for use in court and to extradite offenders.

An overarching trend in the fight against trans-border corruption is universal jurisdiction. This means a country can bring to trial and prosecute in that country those accused of having committed a crime in another country.

The SCORPENE submarine scandal provides the platform for universal jurisdiction to be applied. By ratifying the UNCAC, Malaysia has signaled to the world our willingness to submit to an international framework of cooperation.

THE LONG ARM OF THE LAW

Judge Le Loire after hearing an elaborate testimony from SUARAM, accepted our statement, and promised to proceed with the inquiry with no stone unturned. On the acceptance of the 7 witnesses proposed by SUARAM, the French Judge had asked for the full details of the persons involved, in order to begin issuing subpoenas as he saw fit.

SUARAM lawyer Joseph Breham has further explained that the French court is able to take on several courses of action, in compelling the Malaysian witnesses to assist in the inquiry and the ongoing investigations.

The judge will issue a subpoena in writing on a witness.

Once a subpoena is issued, the witness is obliged to appear before the courts and to assist the courts in its works.

If the witness refuses to abide by the subpoena, the court can issue a notice "mandate d 'amener", compelling the witness to appear before it.

If the witness fails to oblige, a warrant of arrest may be issued. The warrant of arrest is applicable within the boundaries of the French territory, and may be internationalized, if the judge deems necessary.

Based on the judges' discretionary power, they can ask Interpol to issue a red notice i.e an international warrant of arrest.

CRIMINAL INVESTIGATIONS

Following the commencement of the civil case between SUARAM and DCNS, the French authorities have initiated criminal investigations against several top ranking DCNS officials.

The outcome of the investigations could lead to prosecution of several officials linked in the procurement process. Witnesses named in the civil case may also be brought into the suspects list to assist in the criminal probe.

Expose and Findings

SUARAM has had several media conferences back in Malaysia, systematically exposing information and developments of the case. Today's media event in Bangkok has been an inevitable outcome, following the forced deportation of one of two SUARAM lawyers, Mr William Bourdon, last July when he visited Malaysia and spoke at a SUARAM sponsored event, giving a briefing on the developments of the case. SUARAM has had several media conferences back in Malaysia, systematically exposing information and developments of the case. The deportation has signaled a complete snub by the Malaysian authorities over the ongoing inquiry, and have rejected any forms of cooperation thus far.

When SUARAM filed a complaint within the French judicial system, in April 2010, public prosecutors raided the DCNS office, and seized confidential documents, including the procurement contract, bank vaults, invoices and other crucial documentation that allowed for further investigation.

Specific findings from the PARIS PAPERS

Document 97.

The documents seized by the French police include a note for the French Minister of Defense dated 2 June 1999 related to an interview with the Malaysian Minister of Defense and the French-Malaysian diplomatic relationships as far as defense is concerned.

In a document tagged "Malaysia", there is a confidential report regarding PERIMEKAR and TERASASI. The report includes a note on "Retracing the background of negotiations". The note states that pursuant to the major defense contracts between France and Malaysia, there is a requirement that substantial transfer of money has to be channeled to individuals and/or political organizations.

The note specifically states that apart from individuals, the ruling party (UMNO) is the biggest beneficiary. Consultants (company agents) are often used as political network agents to facilitate these monetary transfers and to receive commissions from their mandators.

The note mentions about Mohd Ibrahim Mohd Noor and Razak Baginda as points of reference for political network. The note further states that both Mohd Ibrahim Mohd Noor and Razak Baginda have strong political connections as Mohd Ibrahim Mohd Noor is close to the Finance Minister Daim Zainuddin and Razak Baginda is close to Defence Minister Najib Razak.

The note also explains that by early 2001, Mohd Ibrahim Mohd Noor's influence began to decline following the fall from power of the Minister of Finance, Daim Zainuddin which resulted in the disappearance of Mohd Ibrahim Mohd Noor's name from PERIMEKAR both as shareholder and director which was later replaced by people of Razak Baginda's network. Razak Baginda eventually becomes the main point of reference for political network to facilitate the money transfer.

The noted stated:

"On the contrary, Razak Baginda maintained excellent ties with the Minister of Defense and the Prime Minister. Furthermore, his wife is a close friend of the Minister of Defense's wife. Therefore, Baginda became the centre of the network: Terasasi is linked to Baginda while PERIMEKAR was initially controlled by Mohd Noor."

Previous Expose

Upon returning from France after meeting with Judge Roger Le Loire at Tribunal de Grande Instance on 19 April 2012 and after gaining full access to the investigation papers, SUARAM had exposed two crucial documents: document 87 and 144.

Document 87

The documents seized by the French police from the office of Mr. Henri GIDE (THALES) on 28 May 2010 includes a fax written in English and sent by F. DUPONT dated 1 June 2001 addressed to D. ARNAUD, CCed to BAIOCCO and SAUVAGEOT with "MALAYSIA/SUBMARINE PROJECT" as the subject.

Mr. DUPONT detailed out the chronology of visits and future actions during the journey in Malaysia of which there were various planned undertakings in particular negotiation meetings with the Ministry of Defense and the management members of PERIMEKAR during which two (2) contract proposals would be mentioned (from DCNI to PERIMEKAR as well as between PERIMEKAR and the Malaysian Government).

He finally indicated a meeting with DATO' SRI NAJIB in France on 14 July 2001 with the condition that DCNI offers a maximum sum of USD 1 billion for PERIMEKAR's stay (in France).

Document 144

The prosecutor's office upon instructions had received from THALES International Asia, an envelope on 22 August 2011. The envelope contained:

- A sub folder entitled "C4"

- A sub folder entitled "invoices"

- PDF files

-        A USB thumb drive

Among the crucial documents was the existence of an invoice faxed by TERASASI Sdn Bhd (Company No.524814-P) on 19 September 2004 to Bernard BAIOCCO the then CEO of THALES International Asia. The invoice stated an amount of Euro 359, 450.00 for the purpose of success fees to be paid to Alliance Bank Malaysia Berhad, Branch CP Tower, Seksyen 16, Petaling Jaya, Account No:12109-0-01-3000450-8 and contains a handwritten note in French as follows:

"Razak demande si ce SF peut etre pris en compte assez vite. Le Support Fee suit avec un rapport".

Translation

Razak requests if that SF can be taken into account quite urgently. The support fee follows with a report.

It therefore appears that Thales International Asia could not ignore that the sum paid to TERASASI Sdn Bhd ultimately benefitted Mr Najib Razak the Minister of Defence and/or his consultant Abdul Razak Baginda.

CONCLUSION

SUARAM's call for accountability for this serious crime of corruption has fallen on deaf ears despite its continuous effort to demand answers from the Government of Malaysia. The insistence of our government leaders that French law cannot reach them, speaks volumes of the ignorance coupled with a lack of political will to perform its obligations under the UNCAC.

However, this will not in any way hamper SUARAM's determination to uncover the truth in its pursuit for accountability. By taking up the case on behalf of the Malaysian taxpayers, SUARAM vowed to continue its effort in unraveling the truth as the case proceeds in the French Court in due course.

Again in another ALIRAN article :

Questioning arms spending in Malaysia: From Altantuya to Zikorsky dated 21 April 2011

(http://aliran.com/aliran-monthly/2011-issues/2011-2/questioning-arms-spending-in-malaysia-from-altantuya-to-zikorsky/)

The murder of Altantuya and the Scorpene deal

It took the brutal murder of a Mongolian national, Altantuya Shaaribuu, in 2006 to shock the nation and for questions surrounding the purchase of two Scorpene submarines to be asked in this country and in France. Altantuya, a Mongolian translator, was shot in the head on 19 October 2006 and then blown up with C4 explosives, which are available only from Malaysia's military.

According to testimony in the trial, Altantuya accompanied her then-lover, Abdul Razak Baginda, to Paris at a time when Malaysia's Defence Ministry was negotiating through a Kuala Lumpur-based company, Perimekar Sdn Bhd, to buy two Scorpene submarines and a used Agosta submarine produced by the French government under a French-Spanish joint venture, Armaris. Perimekar at the time was owned by a company called Ombak Laut, which was wholly owned by Abdul Razak. The contract was not competitive.

The Malaysian Ministry of Defence paid 1 billion euros (RM 4.5 billion) to Amaris for the three submarines, for which Perimekar received a payment of 114 million euros (RM510 million). The total cost of the submarines purchase after including infrastructure, maintenance, weapons, etc. has risen beyond RM7 billion. The Deputy Defence Minister, Zainal Abdidin Zin, told Parliament that the money was paid to Perimekar for "coordination and support services" although the fee amounted to a whopping 11 per cent of the sales price for the submarines.

Two former police bodyguards of the then Deputy Prime Minister and Defence Minister were subsequently found guilty of her grisly murder, it raised suspicion of official cover up since their motives were never divulged to the public nor probed in court. Altantuya had had a relationship with Abdul Razak Baginda, a defence analyst from the Malaysian Strategic Research Centre think-tank, with ties to Najib Razak. She had worked as Abdul Razak's translator on a deal to purchase Scorpene submarines from France.

Further in a press statement dated 17 October 2012 released by SUARAM :

PRESS STATEMENT : 17 OCTOBER 2012
SCORPENE INQUIRY:
SUARAM CLARIFIES MISINFORMATION and LIES

"...Investigations so far have provided sufficient evidence to point our fingers at Malaysian officials in the judicial inquiry..."
Joseph Breham, French lawyer

SUARAM has been placed under the microscope of no less than 6 government agencies in recent months, and investigated for various allegations of wrongdoings. Leaders and key staff of SUARAM have been repeatedly summoned to the Companies Commissions and investigated by the police under S112 of the Criminal Procedure Code.

While these agencies have worked overzealously to look for non-existing faults, SUARAM continues to be the target of incessant attacks by GONGOs and pro-government groups alike, mercilessly demonized and tried in the mainstream media for numerous alleged wrongdoings; chief of which are our wide links with foreign interests, being recipients of Soros and other sources of foreign funding as well as registering ourselves as a company instead of a society.

The Barisan Nasional administration has gone into overdrive to discredit SUARAM and delegitimizing us in the eyes of the Malaysian public.

As has always been the case, our heavily skewed mainstream media, has almost never published our right of reply, and we suffer from the barrage of unsubstantiated reports published by them. For a relatively small human rights organization, which has existed for more than 23 years, such disproportionate attacks and bullying reflects the mindset of an insecure and desperate administration, hell bent on silencing critical voices in the lead up to the General Elections.

The last week however has seen the attacks on SUARAM shift from our various alleged wrongdoings, to something more specific : THE SCORPENE CASE. So the real reasons for harassment and intimidation have finally surfaced. SUARAM is being punished and vilified for its role as a whistleblower in the Scorpene case. Instead of investigating the complaints, SUARAM is being investigated instead.

And what better way than to have former French Head of Prosecution, Yves Charpenel who was in town for a conference, to say that there was "no trial" in France.

For ease of reference, Mr Charpenel's statements are reproduced in the following:-

"...The media in Malaysia should be able to distinguish between rumours and facts, and between investigations and a trial..."
"...I am aware about all the fuss kicked up by certain media (organisations) in Malaysia over this but what I can say is that this is nothing more than a trial by the media..."
"...A trial is a trial with all the rules. Investigation is another thing..."

We wish to categorically clarify our position in the following:-

1. It is a fact that the investigations on the Scorpene scandal has commenced. It is not a rumour;
2. All previous statements issued by SUARAM have used the term "judicial inquiry" and "criminal investigations" interchangeably;
3. At no material time has SUARAM used the term "trial" in SUARAM's statements to the public;
4. A trial is different from an investigation;
5. The investigation on the Scorpene scandal is being conducted in Paris and by no way conducted by the media in Malaysia let alone tried by the media in Malaysia;
6. In all of statements in the past, we have maintained very clearly that the complaint filed by SUARAM at the end of 2009, had led

French prosecutors to find sufficient prima facie evidence to allow the inquiry to move into the open courts for a deepened investigation;

7. A judicial inquiry had commenced on 16 March 2012, and SUARAM was made a civil party to the case;
8. The inquiry is being heard at the Tribunal de Grande Instance;
9. Two judges were appointed to preside over the case; Roger Le Loire and Sergie Tournaire;
10. SUARAM had testified before the judge on 19 April 2012;
11. The investigative / instruction judges have the powers to investigate as well as hear witnesses as part of its tasks in presiding over the inquiry;
12. A list of Malaysian witnesses was proferred to the judge who said he will decide on when to call upon these persons as the case develops;
13. The International Federation for Human Rights (FIDH) has no role in the ongoing judicial investigations as alleged by the Young Journalist Club Malaysia, despite SUARAM being a member in the human rights coalition;
14. Mr Charpenel is a former Head of Prosecution;
15. Mr Charpenel has no working knowledge on the Scorpene inquiry;
16. To date, counsel for SUARAM had not been notified by the prosecutors that the Scorpene inquiry will not proceed to a full trial;
17. Mr Charpenel had not been appointed as the prosecutor for the Scorpene inquiry; and
18. Mr Charpenel was commenting on a subject of which he is unfamiliar with and hence, devoid of merit and authority.
19.

At no material time had SUARAM misled the Malaysian public on the progress and facts of the SCORPENE case, as alleged by BN's media.

We reiterate that the French judicial system differs widely from the British / Commonwealth system, hence a proper understanding is needed by discerning Malaysians, in order to understand the developments of the case. SUARAM shall not bear the responsibility of the misunderstandings and deliberate confusion being caused by various parties over the legalities of the case.

Major Elements in the Case

Highlights from the Investigation papers :

Former finance director of DCN, Gerarde Philippe Maneyas had made a claim for 32 million Euros allegedly used to bribe Malaysian officials for purchase of the Scorpenes. We know that at least 32 million Euros were paid by Thales International (Thint) Asia to Terasasi.

There is an invoice by Terasasi dated 1.10.2000 for 100,000 Euros.

There is also an invoice from Terasasi to Thint Asia, dated 28.8.2004 for 359,450 Euros with a hand-written note saying : *"Razak wants it in a hurry."*

With the new French law and OECD Convention against corruption in place after 2002, the French arms merchants had to find a way to pay commissions to their foreign clients. The method used was to create "service providers" that could "increase invoices" in order to take the place of commissions.

Intermediary countries were then used to facilitate payments. The companies used in the Malaysian case were" Gifen in Malta, Eurolux in Luxemburg and Technomar in Belgium. Among the ivoices uncovered were travel expenses of Baginda and Altantuya to Hong Kong and Macau. Parliamentarians in Malta have also questioned their governments for answers over the role of Malta in this case.

Thus, when the French state company DCN terminated its contracts, Thales took over as a private company, not involving the state. Thales International was appointed to coordinate the political connections.

A commercial engineering contract was then signed between DCNI and Thales, referred to as "C5". It covered 30 million Euros in commercial costs abroad. Another "consulting agreement" was signed in 2000 between Thint Asia and Terasasi for 2.5 million Euros.

While we have been told about PERIMEKAR and its role, there has been a pin drop silence on the other company TERASASI. Defence Minister Zahid Hamidi denied having any knowledge on this company in his answers to Parliament last June. The taxpayers have the legitimate interest to know the role of TERASASI however, salient questions relating to the Scorpene scandal were met with silence. Until today, the government had yet to explain to the public the exact role of TERASASI. Perhaps the 6 agencies taskforce set up to investigate SUARAM should utilize its research materials and start looking into TERASASI.

Joseph Breham had in our joint press conference in Bangkok, also uncovered that a secret document was found in the Thales office, belonging to the Royal Malaysian Navy on the proposals linked to the submarines. Was this document sold to Thales with complete disregard to national secrets?

Questions remain unanswered.

Malaysia's Legal Obligations Under the UN Anti Corruption Convention.

Malaysia as a signatory to the UNCAC since 2008, is now obliged to cooperate with other nation states in preventing, investigating and prosecuting offenders of corruption. State parties are bound to render specific forms of mutual legal assistance in gathering and transferring evidence for use in court and to extradite offenders.

An overarching trend in the fight against trans-border corruption is universal jurisdiction. This means a country can bring to trial and prosecute in that country those accused of having committed a crime in another country.

The SCORPENE submarine scandal provides the platform for universal jurisdiction to be applied. By ratifying the UNCAC, Malaysia has signaled to the world our willingness to submit to an international framework of cooperation.

The question is, will the MACC kick-start an investigation on the Scorpene scandal? Can the full facts be told in the Parliament and released to the public?

The attacks launched against SUARAM, as the whistleblower in the Scorpene Inquiry is a reflection of a desperate government who have realized the magnitude and impact of the Scorpene deal. SUARAM reiterates the need for Malaysian public institutions to function independently and effectively in promoting good governance and combating corruption.

Released by,
SUARAM

SUARAM released another press statement dated 23 April 2013 :

PRESS STATEMENT: 23 APRIL 2013

OPS SCORPENE: FRENCH INQUIRY MAKES HEADWAY

On 19 April 2013, 2 SUARAM secretariat, and key spokespersons of the Ops Scorpene campaign, Ms Cynthia Gabriel and Ms Fadiah Nadwa, went on an urgent mission to PARIS at the request of SUARAM's French lawyers, William Bourdon and Apoline Cagnat.

The two judges in charge of the case Roger LeLoire and Serge Tournaire, have been following recent new information offered by various persons on the death of Altantuya Shaaribuu.

The brief mission discussed the following details:

1.   Important revelations on the deepening role of **Najib Razak** in the SCORPENE Scandal and the brutal murder of Altantuya Shaaribuu.
2.   New and damning revelations surrounding the SD1 and SD2, the testimonies of the late PI Bala shortly before his death, on Najib's and his family members direct hand in the controversy and the further revelation of lawyer Americk Sidhu at the Malaysian BAR AGM 16th March 2013.
3.   The lead judge in the ongoing inquiry Roger Le Loire has requested further information on how the recent testimonies will impact upon the ongoing investigations. The French courts have now extended its investigations into circumstances that led to her death,

and especially if Najib had abused his powers as then Deputy Prime Minister to cover the truth behind the brutal death of Altantuya.

4. Ongoing investigations some of which are completely confidential and are awaiting the green light from the judge before it gets to the public domain hopefully in the coming days.

Outcomes

1. Our lawyers have submitted to the judge, the latest developments, suggesting strong elements of acts of criminality under the Penal Code including criminal intimidation and obstruction of justice by Najib in instructing for the SD2 to be formulated, for the fabrication of lies and untruths without the consent of PI Bala.

1. 2 new witnesses will be subpoenaed urgently. The first is senior lawyer Americk Sidhu (PI Bala's lawyer) followed by Cecil Abraham. We note that the Bar Council has just a few days ago reported that they have referred Cecil Abraham to the Advocates & Solicitors Disciplinary Board for misconduct.

2. At least two other fresh exposes will be made in the coming weeks, pending approval from the judge.

BACKGROUND

French prosecutors found prima facie evidence to investigate alleged improprieties against French naval shipbuilder DCNS over its sale of two Scorpene submarines to the Malaysia in 2002. Judges Roger Le Loire and Serge Tournaire – have been entrusted to oversee the case at the Paris Tribunal de Grande Instance.

SUARAM has been made a civil party to the ongoing inquiry, which commenced on 16 March 2012. The two judges are designated to investigate the (alleged) misuse and mismanagement of funds amounting to more than 114.9 million Euros or RM 540 million ringgit.

We thank our lawyers and judge Le Loire for their diligence in pushing open the ongoing inquiry onto new levels, where the investigations will now focus on Najib as a key personality in trying to cover up the death of Altantuya Shaaribuu, and his deepening role in the Scorpene Scandal.

Thank You

Cynthia Gabriel

Fadiah Nadwa

Released by,

SUARAM

In an ensuing SUARAM PRESS RELEASE dated 3 May 2012 http://www.suaram.net/?p=3276 :

SCORPENE SUBMARINE SCANDAL –

THE GREAT MALAYSIAN ROBBERY

In the continuing saga of the **Ops Scorpene** campaign, SUARAM is here today to reveal to you further findings of the ongoing investigations of the French inquiry.

As was reported, the SUARAM delegation comprising Kua Kia Soong, Cynthia Gabriel and Fadiah Nadwa, returned after a successful trip to Paris, and a hearing before judge Roger Le Loire, one of the two Instruction Judges assigned to oversee the French inquiry into the controversial purchase of the 2 submarines by the Malaysian government in 2002.

The judge had principally accepted a list of seven proposed witnesses including current Defence Minister Ahmad Zahid Hamidi, former Defence Minister and current Prime Minister Najib Razak, and a central figure in the procurement process, Abdul Razak Baginda as key witnesses that can further assist in the inquiry before the Tribunal de Grande Instance.

Access to the Investigation Papers

SUARAM has gained full access to investigation papers from the Public Prosecutor's office. This is a huge step forward, as many of the details kept confidential are now made accessible to SUARAM as the Plaintiff in the civil case against the DCNS.

French law provides several constraints on the area of access. While we are not able to obtain a hard copy and distribute copies around, we are however entitled to full view of the documents and are able to quote them to the media and to the public.

It is also to be noted that the complaint lodged by SUARAM has led to the evolution of a criminal investigation which has just commenced which will result in the criminal prosecution of those involved in this corruption scandal. The French, Malaysian officials and the companies involved in the corruption scandal may be put on the suspect list as the criminal case proceeds in the French Court.

Legal Jurisdiction

Judge Le Loire after hearing an elaborate testimony from SUARAM, accepted our statement, and promised to proceed with the inquiry with no stone unturned. On the acceptance of the 7 witnesses proposed by SUARAM, the French judge had asked for the full details of the persons involved, in order to begin issuing subpoenas as he saw fit.

SUARAM lawyer Joseph Breham has further explained that the French courts is able to take on several courses of action, in compelling the Malaysian witnesses to assist in the inquiry and the ongoing investigations.

1. The judge will issue a subpoena in writing on a witness.
2. Once a subpoena is issued, the witness is obliged to appear before the courts and to assist the courts in its works.
3. If the witness refuses to abide by the subpoena, the court can issue a notice "mandate d 'amener", compelling the witness to appear before it.
4. If the witness fails to oblige, a warrant of arrest may be issued. The warrant of arrest is applicable within the boundaries of the French territory, and may be internationalized, if the judge deems necessary.
5. A red alert can be sent to INTERPOL, if the situation warrants based on the discretionary powers of the judge.

New Expose and Findings

In today's media conference we shall focus the expose to two key documents.

1. Document 87

1. Document 144

Document 87

The documents seized by the French police from the office of Mr. Henri GIDE (THALES) on 28 May 2010 which includes a fax written in English and sent by F. DUPONT dated 1 June 2001 addressed to D. ARNAUD, CCed to BAIOCCO and SAUVAGEOT with "MALAYSIA/SUBMARINE PROJECT" as the subject.

Mr. DUPONT detailed out the chronology of visits and future actions during the journey in Malaysia of which there were various planned undertakings in particular negotiation meetings with the Ministry of Defense and the management members of PERIMEKAR during which two (2) contract proposals would be mentioned (from DCNI to PERIMEKAR as well as between PERIMEKAR and the Malaysian Government).

He finally indicated a meeting with DATO' SRI NAJIB in France on 14 July 2001 with the condition that DCNI offers a maximum sum of USD 1 billion for PERIMEKAR's stay (in France).

Document 144

The prosecutor's office upon instructions had received from THALES International Asia, an envelope on 22 August 2011. The envelope contained:

— A sub folder entitled "C4"

- A sub folder entitled "invoices"

- PDF files

- A USB thumb drive

Among the crucial documents was the existence of an invoice faxed by TERASASI Sdn Bhd (Company No.524814-P) on 19 September 2004 to Bernard BAIOCCO the then CEO of THALES International Asia. The invoice stated an amount of Euro 359, 450.00 for the purpose of success fees to be paid to Alliance Bank Malaysia Berhad, Branch CP Tower, Seksyen 16, Petaling Jaya, Account No:12109-0-01-3000450-8 and contains a handwritten note in French as follows:

"Razak demande si ce SF peut etre pris en compte assez vite. Le Support Fee suit avec un rapport".
Translation
Razak requests if that SF can be taken into account quite urgently. The support fee follows with a report.

It therefore appears that Thales International Asia could not ignore that the sum paid to TERASASI Sdn Bhd ultimately benefitted Mr Najib Razak the Minister of Defence and/or his consultant Abdul Razak Baginda.

The Great Malaysian Robbery

It has become apparent that this constitutes one of the Malaysian government's greatest robberies over its people! It is no longer just the

Euro 114.9 million commissions to Perimekar that formed the basis of the complaint to the French Courts that is in question.

It has magnified into a web of lies involving a slew of companies formed to complicate the concealment of the blatant robbery of Malaysian and French tax-payers' money. More retro-commissions have surfaced allowing the misuse of such bodies as the pilgrimage funds (Lembaga Tabung Haji) and the military pension funds (Lembaga Tabung Angkatan Tentera).

The Malaysian and French peoples have been clearly misled, cheated and robbed of their monies through blatant corruption and mismanagement of funds in the name of national secret and security.

SUARAM demands:

1.   The MACC to immediately open an investigation in the light of these new revelations by the French Public Prosecutors.

1.   The full cooperation of the Malaysian government, both moral and legal, into the ongoing inquiry in France.

1.   The Defence Ministry to come clean, and list out to Parliament what other companies were involved in the procurement process and who were the beneficiaries of the kickbacks and commissions.

In another press statement released by SUARAM dated 30 July 2013 :

30 JULY 2013

JASBIR SINGH CHAHL- We want the whole TRUTH behind the SCORPENE SCANDAL

SUARAM views with interest the weekend revelations of Jasbir Singh Chahl, on the SCORPENE Submarine procurement, and welcomes his sudden willingness to speak about the controversial deal, of which he was a key negotiator. We urge him to come clean on the full details of the procurement, which has now dragged on to be one of the largest corruption scandals of the country.

SUARAM had to await confirmation from our lawyers in France, before addressing the media.

1. **1.   JASBIR as Witness to the French Courts**

Firstly, we confirm via our Lawyers in France (William Bourdon and Apoline Cagnat) that Jasbir Singh Chahl is a witness to the ongoing criminal inquiry, and that the investigations are still ongoing. This verification coincides with his own admissions in the NST article that he has been in close contact and has been cooperating with the French investigators. His statement to the NST vindicates further that the SUARAM initiated inquiry at the Tribunal de Grande Instance is making sound progress and is gaining traction.

1.   We remind the press that this is the same man who just last year came out with strong denials that he was involved in the scandal ridden procurement, following SUARAM's expose that he would be among the key witnesses to be called before the French tribunal to testify.

1.   Whatever his motivation to come out of his silence after more than a decade, Malaysians will never know. He has done well by opening a can of worms with his NST interview, and by doing so provoking further interest into the corruption allegations, where after more than a decade, many answers are still left wanting.

Why was JASBIR OUSTED of the DEAL?

1.   **4.**   SUARAM urges Jasbir to take the next step and go all the way to reveal the full details of the procurement, his role in closing the deal, why he was ousted from the negotiations, why did then Defence Minister Najib see it fit to intervene and push his long time friend Razak Baginda into the foray to lead the negotiations instead?

1.   **5.   JASBIR's RM50 million suit against BAGINDA**
It is no secret really that Jasbir had a major fallout with Razak Baginda, as described in the contents of an article published in the Far Eastern Economic review (FEER) back in 2002. A RM 50 million suit was filed by Jasbir , but he eventually settled for an out of court of settlement, according to French investigating papers. SUARAM wonders why none of these details were articulated in the NST article.

6. JASBIR and TERASASI?

What about Jasbir's role in Terasasi Sdn Bhd, and why this mysterious company was never made public? If not for the French investigations, Malaysians would still be in the dark over this. Jasbir is compelled to tell us the exact amounts of money that Terasasi received from French shipbuilders, and what exactly led to its dissolution of the company here and why the subsequent formation in Hong Kong.

7. ALTANTUYA SAARIBUU

On the subject of Altantuya Shaaribu, SUARAM reiterates that we had never described her as a translator. In fact SUARAM has asked repeatedly what was her real role in the submarine deal? It comes as no surprise to read Jasbir's admission that he had never met her, as he was pushed out of the deal midway.

The question that begs to be answered is who is Altantuya , what was her role in the procurement of the submarines if any, and why was she so brutally killed. The French inquiry despite its emphasis on the corruption crimes and kickbacks, have agreed to probe the circumstances around Altantuya's death and whatever connections she could have had with the submarine deal.

PERIMEKAR and the EURO 114.9 million euro

1. Finally, we read with deep interest Jasbir's lame attempt at vaguely doing a breakdown at how the Euro 114.9 million Euros was derived and paid to Perimekar.

We note that Perimekar 's annual statements have shown a tumble since its inception. Between 2009 and 2010, while the submarines were being delivered, Perimekar's activity has slid down: the company has seen its net income decrease from a profit of RM19 million to a loss amounting to RM3.3 million.

The financial report of 2010 stated: "The company's project with the government of Malaysia was completed on Dec 25, 2009, after which a downsizing exercise was done in a fair manner and the company was focusing on prospecting for other viable business opportunities."

Was Perimekar set up just to receive the kickbacks from the Submarine Deal?

Why was Jasbir silent on all of these?

OUR DEMANDS

–   It is clear from Jasbir's interview that the French inquiry is making headway. Many attempts have been made to discredit SUARAM and our lawyers in France, but today we are more than glad to confirm that the French investigators are digging deeper to uncover the truth, and Jasbir has admitted that he has been in constant communications in this criminal inquiry.

– SUARAM demands that the full and whole truth be made known, and for Jasbir to answer the above questions, as his interview in the NST has far from cleared the doubts around the corruption commission and kickbacks. This man as the original negotiator has all the information, and must act with full responsibility to come clean on what actually happened.

– Jasbir and all other witnesses listed cooperate with the French inquiry to bring the truth behind this controversy once and for all.

– For MACC to drop its long and pregnant silence over this case, and open its investigation books. Its really time to nab big fish corruption.

END

Released by,

SUARAM Secretariat

In an article by Malaysiakini dated 1 February 2015 with the headlines "Court Probing Razak's Role in Scorpene Deal" http://www.suaram.net/?p=6944 :

Suaram's case filed in France against French naval company DCNS in 2011, on kickbacks allegedly paid out in Malaysia's RM7.3 billion Scorpene submarine deal, is still "alive" according to a former director of the NGO, Cynthia Gabriel. As the case was filed during her tenure, she still maintains an interest in it.

Gabriel said to the best of her knowledge, the NGO, which filed the case in Paris in 2011, had not abandoned the case.

She said the court was trying to confirm whether political analyst Abdul Razak Baginda, who escaped trial and conviction for the murder of Mongolian national, Altantuya Shaariibuu, had acted in a formal capacity for Malaysia's Defence Ministry.

Gabriel said so far, Abdul Razak, believed to be living in the United Kingdom now, was featured as a "friend or close ally" of Najib Abdul Razak, who at that time was deputy prime minister.

Najib, who is now Malaysia's prime minister, was also defence minister during the procurement of the submarines, for which the deals were inked in 2002.

"There is no certainty that Abdul Razak had acted as a public sector officer. Whether he acted in a formal capacity for the Defence Ministry or as a friend of Najib, is now being determined by the court.

"His role was as the main negotiator in the procurement process," said Gabriel, one of the founders of the Centre to Combat Corruption and Cronyism (C4), an anti-graft watchdog.

She said Suaram had asked several legal bigwigs and professors of law to actually study the case, to determine if Najib's aides, like Abdul Razak, can be subjected to the The Organisation for Economic Co-operation and Development (OECD) convention.

The OECD convention only applies to wrongdoing by public sector officials.

"The Malaysian government should answer and collaborate with the French courts in this matter but so far they have not," Gabriel claimed.

Alleged kickbacks

Suaram had alleged that DCNS paid 114.9 million Euro (RM452 million) in kickbacks to Perimekar Sdn Bhd – a company partially owned by Abdul Razak, in the sale of two Scorpene-class submarines to Malaysia.

Both the government and the "architect" of the deal, one Jasbir Singh Chahl, had defended the Scorpene contract award, saying it was made on a transparent basis to "the technically most qualified party on a commercially competitive negotiated price."

In an interview with Bernama, Jasbir had explained that the contract between the Malaysian government and Perimekar Sdn Bhd was for "defined scope of works", and provision of such services was within commercial norms.

Bernama had reported that Jasbir said Perimekar was nominated as the local vehicle to spearhead the submarine project, while Terasasi Sdn Bhd (TSB) was incorporated to serve as an external service provider to advise and assist Thales.

Jasbir had also claimed that Altantuya, who was murdered by two former bodyguards of Najib in 2006, was not involved when the deal was negotiated and finally signed in 2002.

However, during the initial court case into her murder, Abdul Razak had revealed that Altantuya was his lover, and had come to Malaysia to "blackmail" him.

Her father, Setev Shaariibuu had always asserted that his daughter acted as a translator for Abdul Razak and was allegedly involved in business deals with him.

Last week, the Federal Court upheld the decision of the High Court, to sentence to death two former police special action unit (UTK) members, former chief inspector Azilah Hadri and corporal Sirul Azhar Umar, for Altantuya's murder although the motive for killing her has never been established.

Meanwhile, Gabriel pointed out that the Malaysian Anti-Corruption Commission (MACC) was reported as applying to use the Mutual Legal Assistance Act (MLA) to get help from the French authorities in its probe into the Malaysia's purchase of the subs.

Gabriel also revealed that the court had interviewed three French personnel and is planning to indict two of them; one was the financial director of DCNS, a shipyard builder based in Paris.

"He was found to have abused his power and violated the OECD convention, which prohibits commissions and kickbacks to public officials," Gabriel said.

SUARAM & Cynthia Gabriel have been vindicated for their vigorous endeavours.

Lastly, the facts based on the above articles are lucidly clear and simple :

1) Altantuya Sharibuu was Razak Baginda's lover/mistress,

2) Razak Baginda was the close confidante & adviser to Najib Razak, the then Defence Minister in the procurement of the Scorpene submarines and other arms,

3) According to reports by the French newspaper Liberation, Altantuya found out that one of the parties involved in negotiations, a Spanish company Armaris, had paid out the commissions of 114 million euros for the deal (reportedly one billion euros or RM4.7 billion for the purchase of three submarines). The commission was credited into the accounts of a company controlled by Razak, Perimekar.

4) The ABDUCTION & GRUESOME MURDER/KILLING of Altantuya Sharibuu, was committed by TWO (2) Convicted Killers, Police Bodyguards to the then Deputy Prime Minister & Defence Minister, the present Prime Minister of Malaysia, Najib Razak.

5) THE ENFORCED DISAPPEARANCE & GRUESOME MURDER/KILLING OF ALTANTUYA SHARIBUU, was committed by TWO (2) Convicted Killers, Police Bodyguards to the then Deputy Prime Minister & Defence Minister, the present Prime Minister of Malaysia, Najib Razak.

Thus, the indictment of the arms maker shows that Suaram's suspicion of commissions paid to Malaysian officials in the Scorpene deal is well founded and vindicates SUARAM.

The Scorpene submarines scandal involving suspected commissions paid to Malaysian defence officials in the French submarines sale in 2002 has finally surfaced in the French court with a first indictment issued against the former boss of an international subsidiary of Thales, suspected of having corrupted then defence minister and the present Malaysian Prime Minister, Najib Razak.

Bernard Baiocco, the former president of Thales International Asia (Thint Asia) was indicted before magistrate Roger Le Loire on 15 December or "active bribery of foreign public officials" including Najib Razak, then minister of defense, and one of his advisers, Abdul Razak Baginda, according to the news agency AFP.

The former boss of Thint Asia, together with the Directorate of Naval Construction (DCN) who made the submarines, was also indicted for complicity in misuse of corporate assets.

www.ingramcontent.com/pod-product-compliance
Lightning Source LLC
Chambersburg PA
CBHW070406190526
45169CB00003B/1134